Tim Seibles circa 1971

PRAISE FOR
FAST ANIMAL

One could say that Tim Seibles' sixth volume, *Fast Animal,* is a collection of poems that aims to map the coordinates of maturity, but Seibles is not content to wax philosophically about roads not taken, rather, he opts to enmesh us in experience—both lived and imagined. These poems instruct us that wisdom is most available to us in those moments when we are apt to lose our way. Ranging across the urban thoughtscape, Seibles' poems insist that signposts are all around us; here, in the form of a comic book hero's solemn purpose, there in the memory of a first crush. With poems whose ambling cadences and formal edginess situate the heartrending infatuations of adolescence alongside the shuddering deliberations of middle age, Seibles engenders the lyricism and phrasing to be found in the most affecting rhythm and blues, insisting that it is only by transgressing borders (of ignorance, fear, short-sightedness) that we can discover a universe full of wonder and grace.

—Herman Beavers

In *Fast Animal,* Tim Seibles has reached a new level of sophistication and emotional depth. His tone has nuances that are so subtly and seamlessly woven together that laughter and sorrow are often present in the same poem. Built like one single sustained song, this book is alive with music, ardor and wit that flow in utterances that are uniquely his and his alone. But in *Fast Animal* there is also a new urgency and tender wisdom that speak to—and about—"the great storm/ each man each/ woman walks/ as if beneath/ a second sky."

—Laure-Anne Bosselaar
author of *The Hour Between Dog and Wolf* and *A New Hunger*

"[Seibles] writes with a lucidity of heart and head and soul about all subjects he gets his hands on. His poems are vivid and succinct and have an ease and a grace and wholeness about them . . ."

—Amy Gerstler, Editor of *Best American Poetry*

FAST ANIMAL

ALSO BY TIM SEIBLES

Buffalo Head Solos

Hammerlock

Ten Miles An Hour (chapbook)

Kerosene (chapbook)

Hurdy-Gurdy

Body Moves

FAST ANIMAL

TIM SEIBLES

etruscan press

Etruscan Press
Wilkes University
84 West South Street
Wilkes-Barre, PA 18766
(570) 408-4546

WILKES UNIVERSITY

www.etruscanpress.org

Published 2012 by Etruscan Press
Printed in the United States of America
Cover design by Michael Ress
Cover photo by Starr Troup
Interior design and typesetting by Julianne Popovec
The text of this book is set in Adobe Garamond Pro.

First Edition

11 12 13 14 15 5 4 3 2 1

Library of Congress Cataloging-in-Publication Data

Seibles, Tim.
Fast Animal by Tim Seibles.
    p. cm.
ISBN 978-0-9832944-2-9 (pbk.)
I. Title.
PS3562.I773B87 2011
813'.54--dc22

                          2011005678

This book is printed on recycled, acid-free paper.

For Gil Scott-Heron and Lillian Smith

ACKNOWLEDGMENTS

I would like to thank the following literary journals and magazines in whose pages some of the poems first appeared:

Black Renaissance Noire
Café Review
Cortland Review
Cider Press Review
ElevenEleven
From the Fishhouse
Flint Hills Review
Huizache
Indiana Review
MiPoesias
Ploughshares
Sweet
Tree House

I would also like to thank the following anthologies for including some of the work found here:

Best American Poetry 2010
The Calabash Anthology: So Much Things to Say
The Darfur Anthology
Rainbow Darkness
Villanelles
The Best of Toadlily Press

FAST ANIMAL

FAST ANIMAL

LATER

I don't know what
I'm becoming:
from calm to fear
my mind moves, then
moves. Out there
is the place—streets,
storm drains, stores—
where everybody
goes: I point at that

then *that.* There
are enemies of the world
in the world.
Know what I mean?
I see them on TV.

The birds, the robins
in particular, repeat
a warning I think
I should understand.
All night
they stay in the trees
with their small beaks.

Do they ever really sleep?

If nothing more, they
insist   they *insist*
on something—just like me
behind these windows,
talking alone

as though thinking
isn't loud enough.
Early:
it used to be early
all the time.

I hear my voice
coloring, filling in
and I feel sure
the way a seed
feels sure
shoving a root

into black dirt: you
can't know
what you're becoming

I

BORN

Is this
how it begins:

a cry that
does not know

who's crying: consciousness
filling your head

like smoke—the brain,
a burning house—

first surge of *self*
as a thing

apart: scorched,
the shock

of touch, smell
and somehow

hunger: the need
to have

what you
cannot have

without help—the
unintentional world

wayward,
aloof—then maybe

relief
in someone's arms: is

this
where your heart rises

then tilts:
between hunger

and

the moment
you are fed—

the mind sprung
by want—your mouth:

the first taste, the forgetting

where you are
and what's to come

4 A.M.

I caught the last great caravan of clouds.
City night. Sky like the inside of a skillet

and bright as ghosts, they crossed—not slowly
but unhurried—as if remembering the way

by feel, the way you might touch the wall
of a dark hall at a friend's house late, moving

toward the back porch where you heard the Junebugs
unbuttoning their brass jackets. September.

September: another good summer gone and me
another season older with these streets

wet from a small storm that woke me
to see silver clouds drawn along the sky.

But before that   I had been dreaming: a box
of bottles on the back seat of a car, sunlight

sassing the windshield. A hitchhiker
wearing the bluest baseball cap

you ever saw. I guess I had been
driving and somehow money

was involved, but neither of us knew
how much. We knew the police

were hiding in the church. "But look
how it is," he said, "The road,

I mean, and wide," and the wind stuttered
in the spidery weeds while the asphalt stirred

like a dark sheet under which someone
sleeping had turned over and then,

it was a river   much wider than a road,
with the air barely brushing the trees

the way you might touch the hair of someone
you loved once, stumbling into her

beneath the marquee after a movie. It was
hard smiling the brief embrace, seeing her walk

away, because her walk was the reason
you had tried to meet her five Junes ago—

her smiling voice, the almost sleepy grace
in her gait: you remember scolding yourself

for *wanting* again: you already believed
she would pass through your life—

which she did—like the good season
of a late hour, like a brightness

opening the dark by feel,
the way a blindfolded boy looks

for his friends in his unlit basement—
the quiet so thick he begins to think

they are gone completely   which, in fact,
they are: having one by one

slipped out the back door
where, after some giggles,

they catch the sunset
rubbing brass into their blue jackets

and decide   to just go home
while he traces the walls,

the dusty sofa, the smooth plank
of the ironing board, not knowing his hands

would eventually find the differences
between what moves, what stays and what

was never really there at all.

NOTES FROM BIG BRAH, TOM THE BOMB

Don Juan of Germantown High School, 1967-68

I say, "Tom,
there's this girl—

> He says, *Is she fine like apple wine?*
> *She fine enough to be a friend a'**mine**?*

Her name is Tina—

> *So you wanna give Tina ya weena?*

and Doc's havin' a party—

> *Is she tuned to your station?*
> *She believin' what you fakin'?*

and she's gonna be there—

> *Tell'er you know the way to San José. Tell'er*
> *you gotta graze in her grass.*

> *Tell'er you ♪ ain't too proud to beg. ♪*

> *Yeah, ya gotsta Rock Hudson on'er.*
> *Give'er the movie-star **moon gazer**—*
> *the look of love—say, "My duty*
> ***is*** *your bootie."*

> *Tell'er your peter is sweeter*
> *and ya know how ta treat'er.*

> *Ya gotta sing a little bittle, little brother,*
> *Gotta hit'er witta little bitta Sinatra:*

> *♪ Everybody*
> *loves **my** body   sometime... ♪*

TERRY MOORE

Our moms got us together at *Woolworth's,*
remember? Cheeseburgers. Summertime. 1967:
Twelve years in the world, mostly we burned

for football, to get it and move, to shake anybody
that wanted to bring us down: six points
was all we needed and time to find the future

where we'd be bad-ass superstars. We thought it was
hard, being young with adults running things, and it
got harder   not to think about girls and which words

would bring them close to our hands. Miniskirts:
remember *checkin' the cheese* in study hall—Marna
Evans—we had no idea where those legs could lead.

If it weren't for movies and the legends
of our big brothers we might never have believed
in smooth whispers, long kisses and maybe, even now,

we'd be dreaming only football—the rough touch
of leather tightly laced, grabbed and carried
to a place where men danced with nothing

to explain—the end zone, the promised land—and who
could blame us for craving such a simple destination?
Then came Joanie and for me it was Jane: short hugs,

slow songs, their mouths swimming into our mouths.
Among the Philly brothers, the word was "swag."
Did you swag on her, we'd ask, supposing the wet

dream of lips. *How many times did y'all swag:* so new,
the French kiss, the perfect neighborhood for anyone
as crazy and blue-balled as boys blazing on the verge

of the verge of their lives. Man,

we spent years on the phone daring each other
not to be young, not to be afraid of whatever
sex might mean. That paperback you found, *Nurse*

Nadine—the way she treated her patients: (what
exactly *was* a blow-job   and how long would it be
till we knew?) Our fathers were scary men—younger

than we are now—and ready to make themselves *clear*
without saying anything, especially when we got too cool
to listen, too big to hear. Did they believe in sex

the way we were starting to? Was there some secret living
softly inside their fists? My father loved my mother.
It looked so simple: year after year, the kiss

goodbye after breakfast, the kiss hello about five,
conversation at dinner, TV until time for bed.
It's pretty clear   I didn't know much

about my parents—just that they were usually
nice people and mostly on my side, and this
makes me wonder just how blind I'm gonna be,

'cause these days, I hardly see anything
the way I saw things back then   and, brah,
my eyes are wide open. The NFL will never

see us: I can't do half the moves we used to do—
loose-leg lean, that cutback stutter: short grass
lit beneath our simmering feet—but I'm glad

these forty years have found us still friends,
that we played some football and watched each other
break slowly into men   which is what we are by now,

which was always what we thought we really wanted.

WOUND

Door
in the flesh
leading where: what

exactly does pain
teach? As if time always

lived in the mirror—
as if the past
itself   looked back—
I remember

what they did: I keep
remembering
the way consciousness
turned

like a fast animal
to the blood
on my face: being

awake
suddenly meant something
else. My eyes,

for a second,
caught the hidden
slant   and whatever
happened before

that
also changed

VENDETTA, MAY 2006

*My thoughts are murder to the State and
involuntarily go plotting against her.*
                    —Henry David Thoreau

As if leaving
it behind would
have me lost
in this place, as if

keeping it
could somehow
save me from the
parade of knives,

I have held
my rage on a short
leash like a good,
mad dog whose bright

teeth could keep
the faces of our enemies
well lit. Is it

wrong to hate
the leaders? Am I wrong
to hate their silk
ties and their

secret economies?
Am I wrong? Am I?
Look how they

work the stage
like cool comedians,
ribbing the nations this
way, then that—

gaff after giggle
filling the auditoriums
with the empty
skulls. Maybe this

is the moment
to abandon
metaphor: shouldn't somebody
make *them*

suffer: now that
war is easy money,
won't the reasons
keep coming to see

how well
people die?

    I guess this
is the world
I was born

into: moonlight,
sunshine—kind city

of my mother's lap, my
father   tossing me

up   and catching me—

I remember
the first time I saw

autumn   outside
my window: the colors

came with the smell
of burning

leaves   and starving
in our basement,

the crickets
trying to stave off

the chill, still working
their little whistles
after dark.

        I think, even
then, I knew a season
would come
for us: the wind

tilting slowly, but
suddenly everyone
is under the cold

still holding on
to their wallets
as the government

quietly turns   and day
after day, the terrible stories

cover everything.

MAD POETS VILLANELLE

The sunrise is nice, but the nightside is bad
When light breaks the dawn, a black sky turns blue
I think I know why certain poets go mad

I once rode the cosmos in a suit stitched in plaid
The Earth was my space ship and me, the rough crew
The big light was nice; but the nightside was bad

I can't understand why I can't understand
They learned me some books and their churchery too
It's pretty damn clear why the poets turn mad

It's a bootiful life! Shouldn't sex make us glad?
But the first touch of lips brings the turn of the screw
The first light's good light, but the blindside is bad

Be all you can be like it says in the ad
And do a few things that the Janjaweed do
You can see why the sweet poets run mad

Sometimes I think I've been totally had
I fell for this life 'cause I thought life was true
The daylight's alright, but the sunset is sad

It looks like this chance is all that I had
I say to the mirror, *That just can't be you*
I guess I see why half the people go mad

Maybe if I could just talk to my Dad:
Didn't it seem like your dream would come true?
The sunrise is nice, but the blindside is bad
I think I know why certain poets go mad

ODE TO *THIS* FOR THAT

Was it, was it,
was it a stubbed toe—*ow!*
a gashed knee—*ugh!* that started
all this, this um, um frenzy,
this nervous blur of lips—the, the,
the manic drive to talk back
to those cracked rocks and cruel thorns
upon whose cool sharps
our thin skins first opened:

as if, having no tongue,
each wound made our mouths
accuse the rough souls
of senseless things, as if
speaking   straddled a kind
of relief, a balance between *what
happened* and being,
a *this* for that:

a moon's worth
of babble for a sun's worth
of burn, the near-words
blurted like insane
punctuation, *aiyeee!*
while the world's over-
whelming everything
flung its wild-ass run-on
smack into our bug-eyed,
bicameral brains,

as if blood—the color,
blood, the trouble
with blood—
would always be more
than speech could prove:

and what about the
elemental hunger
for sex: *ahh*—the wanton
selection of human
moves, the heart's groan
held gut-deep

when some someone
slowly sways past, *unh*—
and the anguish
left in their wake: the moment
when craving
first pronounced its name, *unh*.

And then   the sky, there
but not there—that, that tease,
heaven,
the absolute
escape, and the word
sky—bright note
filling your mouth
as if that sound
were a taste of the blue
blue called up
by the one star building
its bodacious light
above the earth—*bodacious*!

O consonants! O vowels!
Such sweet, early animal music:
before you were there,
you were there
with those first tiny voices,
even the insects—*ch-ch-ch*—
trying to speak
and now, the outrageous
human fracas: *Greedy*
Peter be-bopped a glass bag
of spackled fractals:
what!? And me

scratching black marks
on blank paper, meaning
to say *this*
about that, and even
this poem: proof
of nothing but the thing
I am, the two-legged, big-
headed, brown-breasted,
half-blind thing
I am   and still
my mouth flies open
as if   but *still!*

FAMILIAR

Some are marked, some…

So many words, such fever: the names
of the strained inhabitants moving

around, waiting   to be called—
my own life: the bending

of a man into something
else: did I change? Are you

changed? I'm sure
it happens. Yes, I believe it

has happened:

II

*Years ago, a pregnant woman was bitten by a vampire
and turned. Her son was born with the thirst
but, being half human, he could walk in sunlight
unharmed. Though vampires quietly dominate the
world, he fights them—in part to prove his allegiance
to humanity, in part to avenge his long isolation, being
neither human, nor vampire. Because of his deadly
expertise and weapon of choice, they call him:*

BLADE, THE DAYWALKER

Like a stake
in my heart: this life—

the seen,
the unseen—the ones

who look in the mirror
and find nothing

but innocence   though they stand
in blood up to their knees.

You see them: shadows
not shadows, people who seem

to be people. You don't
believe me? I watch

their news, drink coffee
in their chains.

There's no place
they haven't touched:

it's almost like I can't
wake up, like I'm living

in a movie, a kind of dream:
action-packed thriller.

I never
dreamed this

hunger in my veins, this
mind that cannot sleep: why

do I whet this blade,
when they will not die.

WHAT

Curiosity: seed
that turns the world
into what

we are
told
by those who
were told
by still others
what's what: The
Telling,

the great storm
each man each
woman walks
as if beneath

a second sky—*this*
and this of course
and this—the rain

rains down
like rain
everywhere
and all over

we don't
know that
we don't

know
what's been
done to us:
consciousness

kept like a fly
in a jar, a small
hope   buzzing the glass:

What is it,
what—
is it, what—
what is it?

DAWN

for Jim Simmerman

So, I thought about death and the dying
it requires   and the idea of lying
face-down somewhere: I thought

it's just too much—the not
knowing, the anytime anyplace
of it: my heart running

out of gas—*me*: tagged
by a bus—my well-meaning self
clipped in the urban crossfire.

Or the giving up on everything,
the world a banquet of good reasons
for clocking out and chomping the black
sandwich. But I thought *but*

there's so much I want
to do, so much I need
to say, so much, so much, *so
mothafuckin' much*   and *Fuck Death*!
And it kept getting later and it was later

than I thought and I thought
about thinking like this, as if
my part were   different,
as if upon my life hung
the balance of good and truth
and fun on Earth: I thought *Shit*!

I'm just a big insect, a giant moth
with teeny-weeny wings! And I
shut up   and I looked out

and the edge of the world began to glow.

DELORES JEPPS

It seems insane now, but
she'd be standing soaked
in schoolday morning light,
her loose-leaf notebook,
flickering at the bus stop,
and we almost trembled

at the thought of her mouth
filled for a moment with both
of our short names. I don't know
what we saw when we saw
her face, but at fifteen there's
so much left to believe in,

that a girl with sunset
in her eyes, with a kind smile,
and a bright blue miniskirt softly
shading her bare thighs   really
could be *The Goddess*. Even
the gloss on her lips sighed
Kiss me   and you'll never

do homework again. Some Saturdays
my ace, Terry, would say, "Guess
who was buying Teaberry gum
in the drugstore on Stenton?"
And I could see the sweet
epiphany still stunning his eyes

and I knew that he knew
that I knew he knew   I knew—
especially once summer had come,
and the sun stayed up till we had
nothing else to do but wish
and wonder about *fine sistas*

in flimsy culottes and those *hotpants!*
James Brown screamed about: Crystal
Berry, Diane Ramsey, Kim Graves,
and *her.* This was around 1970: Vietnam
to the left of us, Black Muslims
to the right, big afros all over my

Philadelphia. We had no idea
where we were, how much history
had come before us—how much
cruelty, how much more dying
was on the way. For me and Terry,
it was a time when everything said

maybe, and maybe being blinded
by the beauty of a tenth grader
was proof that, for a little while,
we were safe from the teeth
that keep chewing up the world.
I'd like to commend

my parents   for keeping calm,
for not quitting their jobs or grabbing
guns   and for never letting up
about the amazing "so many doors
open to good students." I wish

I had kissed
Delores Jepps. I wish I could
have some small memory of her
warm and spicy mouth to wrap
these hungry words around. I

would like to have danced with her,
to have slow-cooked to a slow song
in her sleek, toffee arms: her body
balanced between the *Temptations'*
five voices and me—a boy anointed

with puberty, a kid with a B
average and a cool best friend.
I don't think I've ever understood
how lonely I am, but I was

closer to it at fifteen because
I didn't know anything: my heart
so near the surface of my skin

I could have moved it with my hand.

ODE TO MY HANDS

Five-legged pocket spiders, knuckled
starfish, grabbers of forks, why
do I forget that you love me:
your willingness to button my shirts,
tie my shoes—even scratch my head!
which throbs like a traffic jam, each thought
leaning on its horn. I see you

waiting anyplace always
at the ends of my arms—for the doctor,
for the movie to begin, for
freedom—so silent, such
patience! testing the world
with your bold myopia: faithful,
ready to reach out at my
softest suggestion, to fly up
like two birds when I speak, two
brown thrashers brandishing verbs
like twigs in your beaks, lifting
my speech the way pepper springs
the tongue from slumber. O!

If only people knew the unrestrained
innocence of your intentions,
each finger *a cappella*, singing
a song that rings like rain
before it falls—that never falls!
Such harmony: the bass thumb, the
pinkie's soprano, the three tenors
in between: kind quintet times two

rowing my heart like a little boat
upon whose wooden seat I sit
strummed by Sorrow. Or maybe

I misread you completely
and you are dreaming a tangerine, one
particular hot tamale, a fabulous
banana! to peel suggestively,
like thigh-high stockings: grinning
as only hands can grin
down the legs—caramel, cocoa,
black-bean black, vanilla—such lubricious
dimensions, such public secrets!
Women sailing the streets

with God's breath at their backs.
Think of it! No! *Yes*:
let my brain sweat, make my
veins whimper: without you, my five-hearted
fiends, my five-headed hydras, what
of my mischievous history? The possibilities
suddenly impossible—feelings
not felt, rememberings un-
remembered—all the touches
untouched: the gallant strain

of a pilfered ant, tiny muscles
flexed with fight, the gritty
sidewalk slapped after a slip, the pulled
weed, the plucked flower—a buttercup!
held beneath Dawn's chin—the purest kiss,
the caught grasshopper's kick, honey,
chalk, charcoal, the solos teased

from guitar. Once, I played
viola for a year and never stopped

to thank you—my two angry sisters,
my two hungry men—but you knew
I just wanted to know
what the strings would say
concerning my soul, my whelming
solipsism: this perpetual solstice
where one + one = everything
and two hands teach a dawdler
the palpable alchemy
of an unreasonable world.

BLADE, HISTORICAL

It is possible that God exists, but with everything
that has happened to us, could it possibly matter?
                              —Mario Vargas Llosa

You come into the world—
from where *from where*—
and the world turns

toward you, fangs bared,
disguised as what it is, as if
this is how it has to be:

as if it were normal to walk
the daylight knowing
something's wrong. *Grow up,*

they say, *get a job, go to church.*
And after awhile you stop
fighting it and try to smile.

Don't you ever wonder
whose blood is in
the banks? It's yours.

Follow the money
back to the Plague and
the rise of the papacy:

The Inquisition. *The Burning*
Times. The explorers
and the *explored.* So many

centuries, so much
death: you can still taste it
on the wind. Some days

I think, with the singing
of my blade, I can fix
everything—even the sadness

that says nothing that matters
will change. Some days
I think I should never have been.

PUNCHING VILLANELLE FOR THE W, 2005

This late has gotten later and my soul begins to slouch
I used to think the future had been waiting up for me
We rumble all around the world and then we stumble out

A broken head, a breaded heart, some lynching north and south:
Ten grains of sand inside one clam—ten pearls I'd sing for free
I stumbled in and played some verbs, but soon I'll stumble out

I tell myself to celebrate—*the sky's a rainbow trout*!
A glance, a smile, a chance of hearts: a whelming kiss to be
But blight has burned the furnace and my soul begins to slouch

I'd like to meet the President   and punch him in the mouth
Sometimes my blood ran thick with words—I meant to sing us free
I ramble everywhere I go, but soon I'll grumble out

Now, half the days I guess my face and act like there's no doubt
Do shadow shapes that branches make mean something to the tree?
This stark begins to darken and my heart begins to crouch

The teams, the games, the superstars—the happy fans all shout!
I sang inside the Spider's house pretending to be free
We bumble all around this place and then they take us out

I think I thought most everyone just wanted to hang out
A pleasant walk, some pleasant talk: the door, the trusty key!
But war plays on in Baghdad and my soul slumps on the couch

If I could kiss Life on the lips I'd love Her till she wheezed
And then I'd buy the world a *Coke* and dump it in the street
We fumble all the days we get and then they give us gout
But first let's meet the President   and slug him in the mouth

THE LAST DRAGON

In this 1985 film, Bruce Lee-Roy must face Sho'Nuff, Harlem's
Shogun, in order to reach the "final level" and get "the glow."

Alas, friends, it is not
The Shogun
of Harlem who knocks
down my sleep
and stomps on my dreams.
Though I must admit
any man
who could walk New York
in red-satin baggies
and blue-velvet shoulder pads

would be a bad brotha
indeed—someone
to whom
I would gladly defer
if we both flagged
the same taxi
one rainy, uptown
afternoon.

Such a man might easily
be misunderstood, could be
in fact, a frustrated
saint, a shaman
with a bad attitude,
who bends the weather
with a smile

some might call
sinister. Maybe he's
just a little
mad
because The Blame
is dressed in everything
and needs no *Converse
All-Stars* to stylize
its callous feet.

The situation *is* desperate.
If he's ready to kick
every ass in Harlem, who
can blame *Sho'Nuff*
for his pure ambition,
for his big heart that swole
from a bruise?

But *Bruce Lee-Roy*:
heroic counterpoint
to cruelty, shy do-bee
of friendly deeds, how
could a black man
like this   walk
among us? Decked out,
like the only brotha
ever born in Beijing,
the sunlit crown
of his coolie hat stuns
the stammering streets. He is

innocence incandesced
in a brown skin. He's

the story almost
never told: a baby-faced
warrior for cultural transcendence—
a true-blue dancer
of the Tao, his body
a weapon
of last resort. Maybe

he knows *Sho'Nuff*
is really his own
meaner self—the Mr. Hyde
to his Dr. Jekyll—
the merciless edge
that sparkles
behind his faithful eyes.

When they meet
in the abandoned factory,
alone together at last,
the clash
is cataclysmic: red lightning
alive in the Shogun's fists
blasting our hero

door to door, wall then floor
until the good Bruce
finds himself finally
awake—his being ablaze
with the golden
sublime,
thus beginning
the greatest comeback
ass-whuppin of all time.

Yo, Lee-Roy, what
wouldn't I do
to turn myself
into you, to catch
the bullet and get up
holding the hollow-point
still hot
between my teeth.

If I could ever
get the glow
I would knock Evil
all the way
to Seventh Heaven.
I'd end the wars
and shine my soul
like a yellow-brick road.
Oh, to *know*

without knowing
how to be
and not to be
afraid

of what life is
and what
I am.

III

ALLISON WOLFF

Like a river at night, her hair—
the sky starless, streetlights
glossing the full dark of it:
Was she Jewish? I was seventeen,

an "Afro-American" senior
transferred to a suburban school
that held just a few of us.
And she had light-brown eyes

and tight tube tops   and skin
white enough to read by
in a dim room. It was impossible
not to be curious.

Me and my boy, Terry, talked about
"pink babes" sometimes: we watched
I Dream of Jeannie and could see Barbara
Eden—in her skimpy finery—lounging

on our very own lonely sofas.
We wondered what white girls were
really like, as if they'd been raised
by the freckled light of the moon.

I can't remember Allison's voice
but the loud tap of her strapless heels
clacking down the halls is still clear.
Autumn, 1972: Race was the elephant

sitting on everybody. Even
as a teenager, I took the weight
as part of the weather, a sort of heavy
humidity felt inside and in the streets.

One day, *once upon a time,* she laughed
with me in the cafeteria—something
about the Tater Tots, I guess,
or the electric-blue Jell-O. Usually,

it was just some of us displaced brothers
talkin' noise, actin' crazy, so she
caught all of us way off-guard. Then,
after school, I waved   and she smiled

and the sun was out—that 3 o'clock,
after-school sun rubbing the sidewalk
with the shadows of trees—

and while the wind pitched the last
of September, we started talking
and the dry leaves shook and sizzled.

In so many ways, I was still a child,
though I wore my seventeen years
like a matador's cape.

The monsters that murdered
Emmett Till—were they everywhere?
I didn't know. I didn't know enough
to worry enough about the story
white people kept trying to tell.

And, given the thing that America is,
maybe sometimes such stupidity works
for the good. Occasionally,

History offers a reprieve, everything
leading up to a particular moment
suddenly declared a mistrial:
so I'm a black boy suddenly

walking the Jenkintown streets
with a white girl—so ridiculously
conspicuous   we must've been
invisible. I remember her mother

not being home and cold Coca Cola
in plastic cups and the delicious
length of Allison's tongue   and
we knew, without saying anything,
we were kissing the *color line*

goodbye   and on and on for an hour
we kissed, hardly breathing, the light almost
blinding whenever we unclosed our eyes—
as if we had discovered the dreaming door
to a different country   and were walking

out   as if we *could* actually
walk the glare we'd been
born into: as if my hand
on her knee, her hand
on my hand, my hand
in her hair, her mouth
on my mouth   opened
and opened and opened

BLADE, UNPLUGGED

It's true: I almost never
smile, but that doesn't mean

I'm not   *in love*: my heart
is that black violin
played slowly. You know that

moment late in the solo
when the voice
is so pure   you feel
the blood in it: the wound

between rage
and complete surrender. That's
where I'm smiling. You just
can't see it—the sound

bleeding perfectly
inside me. The first time
I killed a vampire   I was

sad: I mean
we were almost
family.

But that's
so many lives
ago. I believe

in the cry that cuts

into the melody, the strings
calling back the forgotten world.

When I think of the madness
that has made me   and the midnight
I walk inside—all day long:

when I think of that
one note   that breaks
what's left of what's
human in me, man,

I love   everything

LOVE POEM

for Renée

Something like soft light, something
like shadows:

> This silence, this
> pause before the machines
> begin again:

earlier than dawn, almost
awake   consciousness remembering

consciousness—itself a dream   near the surface
of things—always invisible, the ghost

moving me around:

> *Hello,* it seems to say,
> *be with me*   but I'm
> not sure.

Alone and not alone, all day
I move around, my heart knocking
against itself.

I think about the perfect agreement
between our bodies, the alliance of hips—

paradise. Our veins
mapped together for awhile:

We have traveled so much
of the territory between us
and still there is a long, long way.

Is this what love is?

On my own, I talk to people.
I turn the same corners with my blood
awake in its maze.

Hello,

I keep trying to say,
but that's not what I mean.

KISS MY VILLANELLE

A blues for James Blood Ulmer

I'm older today than I was yesterday
And somehow I guess I jus' done lost the knack
I wish I could fix that, but what can I say?

I trundle around with my feet made of clay
You'd think after'while y'all might cut me some slack
I'm older today than I felt yesterday

If Sade Adu called, I'd go right away
I bet she keeps love in a black satin sack
I wish I could meet her, but what can I say?

Don' look over here like I'm just in the way
Time was the fine girls kept me flat on my back
I'm older today than I did yesterday

I pagan the streets with my heart like a stray
And hum with the trees till the sweet Earth hums back
Don' wanna be lonesome, but what can I say?

When I get the good cards, you jus' mess up my play
Would you kiss my behind if I sat on a tack?
I'm bolder right now than I'll be in a day

How can I help but get carried away?
When I was a boy I got beat with the strap
I try to forget that, but what can I say?

It takes more than guts to go jump in the fray
I spit in the wind and the wind spits right back
It's colder today than it was yesterday
I wish I could fix that, but what can I say?

SORROW

It's not the same
as sadness, though sorrow
has sadness in it—the way *lost*

holds losing: you can see it
in women's eyes when they laugh
and in the way men lean

over their food: after awhile,
we know nearly every love
won't go as it should,

and we know that knowing
cannot make us glad: *knowledge*
stairway to nowhere—we want

the world we cannot have,
and every day the feeling moves
between us, but we try

not to complain and almost
never fall down and cry.

A FUNKY BLUES

for Carrie and Lurrie Bell

The night dark
as the unplayed B-side
of a Motown flop. Seem like
the whole world a broken record
stuck on *same ol' same ol'*.
And here come a piece a'moon
skinny as Darlene's leg
droppin light
like chump change
on my corner—a moon that
need its sorry butt kicked,
jus like cool-ass Jerome
comin'round in wrinkled shirts
and mismatched socks,
lookin' *hongry*, steady tryin
to borrow somethin and
"pay you back later."

I 'member one time
I let that mahfucker hold $25
"till next Tuesday"—*$25!*
Like I got that many beans ta burn:
musta been feelin like Jesus or somethin.
Well, *next Tuesday* been and gone
prolly twenty-five times by now,
and if I seen a penny a'that money
I mus got Halle Berry upstairs
in a satin teddy too.

My whole life been a
night like this: dark so old
the stars be wheezin
and never nobody around
that I wanna see: light fallin
a little bit here,
a little bit there, but mostly
a whole lotta *shoulda-coulda*
comin down my street
up to no good, steady ready
to get somethin and
never give nothin back.

EDGE

Traffic: solitude,
the city—walking around.

So many of us lost in it.
Is love the secret

nobody tells? In a small park
daylight pulled its knife

and a tree moved
toward me: *What are you*

doing here?
I remembered then: I lit

my eyes   which had
gone out

✗ BLADE, UNSYMPATHETIC

They *don't matter; they're our* food.
                                        —Deacon Frost

Ever take *Communion*? Ever
watch the war on TV? This place
is for predators, baby.
It doesn't matter
that you never knew:
your innocence

is the key they turn
to let you out
and lock you in. Nobody
wants to see
what's

really happening—
and by the time you
start to understand,
the baby teeth are gone
and the big teeth
come in: you're in
the blood

and the blood's   on you.
If you play along
almost everyone will
sort of
be your friend: in the
human world,
don't the wolves look a lot
like the sheep

before the slaughter
begins? Try to remember:
is that *your* face
in the window? Is that
your name on the card?

Maybe you should get
some body armor. What else
can I say? Mine is black.
Eat as much garlic
as you can.

IV

✗FAITH

Picture a city
and the survivors: from their
windows, some scream. Others
walk the aftermath: blood
and still more blood coming
from the mouth of a girl.

This is the same movie
playing all over
the world: starring everybody
who ends up where the action
is: lights, cameras, close-ups—*that*
used to be somebody's leg.

Let's stop talking
about *God*. Try to shut-up
about heaven: some of our friends
who should be alive   are no longer alive.
Moment by moment death moves
and memory doesn't remember,

not for long: even today—even
having said
this, even knowing that
someone is stealing
our lives—I still
had lunch.

Tell the truth. If you can.
Does it matter   who they were,
the bodies in the rubble: could it matter

that the girl was conceived by two people
buried in each other's arms, believing
completely in the world between them?

The commanders are ready. The guns
walk everywhere. Almost all of them
believe in God. But somebody should

hold a note   for the Earth,
a few words for whatever being

human   could mean
beneath the forgotten sky:

some day one night,
when the city lights go out for good,

you won't believe how many stars

DONNA JAMES

I remember that first time:
the empty auditorium, her voice,
the dark all around us,
her mouth reaching into mine.
She was Freddy's foxy older sister,
and I didn't know why
she wanted to kiss me. She
had already finished high school
and probably shouldn't have
been walking the halls, but
she always called me her *friend*.
So one Monday after gym,

I found myself beside myself
in front of her house—with my
trench coat and lunch bag—
probably *not* looking much
like Shaft. Inside, the air held
warm milk and we talked a bit
about her baby   and her Aunt
who paid the rent painting cars.

Maybe she liked me because
we were both black and mostly
alone in the suburbs, but I hadn't
thought about that. It was her voice
that got me—banked fire, the color
of dusk—her voice, and my name
was smoke in her mouth.

I think about it more than I should now,
that January noon—an hour before
algebra—how most days I'd be
thinking football   or replaying
the seventy-some kisses I'd gotten
over those lean years, but that day

Donna and me were on the couch
munching potato chips. *Rrruffles
have rrridges,* she kidded coming
from checking the baby who'd
slipped into a nap. I was kind of
disappointed that we hadn't
done anything, but I needed time
to get back to school, so I started
to stand. She said *wait,
look at this mess,*

and with her left hand, she
brushed the crumbs from my lap
the way you'd whisk away lint—
then, swept over my pants again—
to be thorough, I guessed, but slower
and then some more, as if her hand

were getting   drowsy. You know
how sometimes you see something
but just can't believe it—like a squirrel
bobbling a biscuit on your kitchen counter
or a cricket creeping the red feathers
of your mother's Sunday hat?

Her hand *there*, on my lap,

could easily have been a five-fingered
flying saucer from the fifth dimension.
For awhile, I just watched and
wondered if she knew where
her hand had landed   but it was me
who didn't know: me with my
six dozen kisses and the great Eden
of my virginity. How
do we not talk about it

every day: the ways
we were changed
by the gift
in someone's touch—your body,
suddenly a bright instrument
played by an otherwise
silent divinity.

When I heard my zipper, I couldn't
have said where my arms
were   or what a clock was for:
I had
no idea   I could be such a stranger
and still be myself. How could I
have known what a girl

might do to a boy
with her mouth   if she felt
like doing what her mouth
could do? It was
a kind of miracle: the dreamed
impossible—my soul finally called
to my flesh. I didn't know
what I didn't know   and then I knew.

ODE TO SLEEP

Like a slight breeze brushing
my hand, a short season
drying a damp room, like
a lost animal, a good
ghost   you come back
and carry me:
my face, a scuffed rose,
my belly prowling, this
brain, a wrinkled suitcase
crammed with old cartoons.

Sleep, when it's late,
when my mind is all
yips and swerves, you
flip me over your shoulder
like a four-year-old
in a sailor suit, over your arm
like a moth-eaten coat.
It doesn't matter where
the day has gone.
You take me back

to the *un*time
where we are never
alone   where *Someone*
always calls me
away from this long
sentence, this
blue circus riding
the sky river—*for what,*

until when?
You let me go
as if I were only a dull whim,
a team of germs, a bent
wheel on the day's
flying bus.

How many lives
run to you   for this
pure chance, that
drowsy touch, your
soft amnesia—think of it!
At any moment, half
of humanity blind
and bundled on your back,
snoring like
there's nothing else
to do—as if that
ragged song
told the only story
that might let us
start again—and still
I forget to thank you.

Sleep,
thank you for the good turn,
for bringing me around
even when you know
I'm burning to stay up:
my heart, that singed
fanatic all the time
running me down
with a few suggestions—

where I should go,
who I might see, *what
we could do!* Once,

dark, dark at night,
I went to bed
with a woman's red hair
so bright
in the middle
of my brain   I thought
I might never
find you:
behind my closed eyes,
her bare legs
blazed beneath her
brown skirt.

But you, You finally
drifted in
with a lazy wave
with no explanation,
saying *let's go*,
and for a little while,
I was nowhere
and you stayed with me.

FROM DARKNESS

Sunrise runs
a fresh wind through the leaves,
a night turns
back into shadows.

Waking up, the birds tell
first light
everything they know.

Why do we keep
killing each other?

The Earth is a woman

who walks
in the sky, *walks
in the sky*!   Her legs
so long

you can't even see them.
For no reason, the morning comes

back again, saying *Come back—
open your eyes.*

BLADE, EPIPHANY

No matter what, the light still burns: in a mirror
they see what they need to see / I find this anger
shaped like a man—as if I stood with the night
climbing my back, as if my human self were better

forgotten. Once, I'd have given anything
to be another face in the glass, another glum grin
getting ready for work, busy enough to lose everything

but my watch—time scrubbing my life
till it fades, time running my brain like a bug
on a hotplate—in too big a hurry to catch the vampires
picking their teeth. People break down so fast.

How can you stand it: you never know
how young you are. All of a sudden, puberty,
then gray hair and a stiff back and the knowledge

that your heart was another place you'd been
forced to leave. And all these years, I thought
I wanted to be human. Maybe I've already lived
too long, but I guess I'll fall for the next life

just like I fell for this one, which seemed
so beautiful at first—like this country
before it was bitten. Is this a life:

stuffing your mouth, chasing the hours,
tracing yourself from daylight to dark?
Is this what you meant when you
said the word *free*? And children get

sent to school—books and books—as if
they could ever learn enough to escape
the *Happy Meals.* I don't know how

to save anybody from this. Centuries pass.
The Earth bleeds by a trillion stars, giving
one side then the other to the blinding sun. So,

I am fighting for what? The right to live
without memory: the right to sing
a-ra-pa-pum-pum every December

with the living dead strumming
their coupons? What could I say
if I woke up in a mirror and found

someone *busy*   looking back: hoping
for a holiday, getting more
and more to do

DANCING VILLANELLE

I guess nobody ever really stands a chance
Man, even the good guys wind up dead
But shouldn't we dance, shouldn't we dance?

I caught the mean truth in a mid-life glance
The friendliest innocence is finally bled
Parents must know kids don't stand a chance

These long-legged women got me looking askance:
Is monogamy honestly better instead?
Let's all of us dance! Couldn't we dance?

I wish Mom had warned me a bit in advance
For the rest of my life, I'll be face-down in bed
You learn to accept that a man's got no chance

I'd like to receive a nice blow-job in France,
a touch of détente to help beat back the dread
If you ask real nice won't they stand you a chance?

Suppose I show up and just take off my pants?
There's a good chance I'd get kicked in the breads
But couldn't we dance? Shouldn't we dance?

Let's work like zombies, walk malls in a trance,
and buy all the bullshit they shine in our heads
Why even wake up if they won't let you dance?

I'm gripping the wheel with both of my hands
Wherever you go the clocks wring out the dead
I guess nobody ever really stood a chance
But didn't we dance, didn't we?

THE LAST POEM ABOUT RACE

Just whistling at white legs once
upon a time, could get a black man
torn apart by some giddy mob tipsy
with their fair skin and cold beer—
and there'd be picnics while he swung
and some singing in the round.

But back then is not now, and the future
is a ditty I hum to myself the way
a child might whistle Dixie just to keep
from hearing what teethes in the dark,
and for most of my life, I have lived there:
belonging and not belonging to America—

this fat animal shape on the globe
where white people have done so much
to so many and get "pretty tired
of hearing about it." I'm not
trying to be mean. I've got
some white blood in my veins—

and really, *whiteness* is just a shadow

of its former self, but still, I'm kinda
scared, confused about what to do
with History while I'm sitting in a park
in Virginia   holding a white woman's hand.
I never want to think being American
is impossible, but the truth is

some silly mothafuckas still fly
Confederate flags   and maybe it's all
too much for any one man. I would like
to say she smiles a smile that locks
the door on grief, that her legs
could make a new priest pause, that

what is unsaid—in the meeting
of our complicated skins—is itself
a word: felt but never defined
exactly   like Time, the way it
shoves everybody forward, then
leaves all of us way behind.

I remember kissing Karen Stickney
in *kidneygarden*, her hair vaselined and wavy,
her buttery brown cheek damp against my lips
how, for the rest of the day, my little brain whistled
like a wiffle ball, though the teacher did make me
stay after school. I told Karen I would save her

if she fell down a hill—and I meant it,
as much as a five-year-old can. Now, fifty years
deep into this, that's mostly what I'm looking for:
a touch of daylight with someone who can turn me
away from the tilt of my own nervous humming.

But what can I say to the black woman
who gives me that hard stare, who cannot hear
my heart crooning, *Of course, I love sistas,*
but isn't everybody beautiful?
In so many ways, the blood is still wet
on the lash   and I see black bodies

everyday pressed into capital—Army, Navy,
NBA, NFL—and who gets to live inside them
lovely new prisons? It must be a riddle
being white, knowing and not knowing what's
what: afraid of the dark citizens but so in love
with that funky music. Even this

slyly freckled woman who squeezes my hand,
whose white skin hides her own hard story,
breathes an air   I can't quite fit into my lungs,
though we groove to *Parliament*
and she throws her hips hard enough
to shake the centuries loose.

I want to believe love can be big enough
to beat back all the bad news, and today
I don't think I do, but maybe I think too much,

and a touch of lips *is* bigger than History,
and where I am, this present tense, is just a song
that's really over   by the time it begins.

CALL

Falling asleep isn't
       falling: your eyelids

meet after all day being
       held apart by the light

we breathe into words:
       the names—for seen,

for unseen: what we call

"awake" brings mostly this
       chatty stupor, this

thinking around: what we call the
       world cannot be found

in the world: breath by breath
       the *said* hides the real

in its glare: the mind is

right to be sick
       of the noise we make:

each night when eyes close,
       consciousness

dreams itself

free: the government
       of the tongue

dissolved, all memory
       scattered   into everything

A SONG

From little Kathleen's note

I hope that we will meet again
if we meet again
I hope

we will meet again
if we meet
again   There was
so much

I didn't say
this time   I hope we will
meet again if we

meet again   Will day break
night again
when we meet again

I won't be this
afraid again
when we meet
again   Won't that

be something
if we meet again
I will play again

when we
meet again if you'll
meet again   I won't

sleep again if we meet again

I hope we meet again

Shouldn't we
meet again
if we meet again   What

could I say
if we met again   The water
would be sweet
again if we met

again   Won't the trees
be tall again if we
climb again

Would it be
here again if we met
again
Maybe we could try
to meet again

Or is again
not like again
I swear

we will meet
again if we meet again
Don't you think

we'll
meet again

when we meet
again   I hope we
can meet
again   Will you
know that we've met
again if we

meet again when we
meet again   Would again
seem like again
again   I hope
we will meet again

if we meet
again once we meet
again   I hope
we will meet again

THE VIEW

As if I'd been stolen
from myself—
                    as if my
Self had somehow been

subtracted—
and I was left with this,

this worried, balding man.

I watch him: getting
under my shirts, into my skin.

Is it time?

                    His eyes,
from the glass, look
almost happy—almost
past me:

                    as if I were blocking
the view, as if my life

had been re-cast
and it was just
a matter

of days   until he shoved me
aside, until I took my
big ideas
                    and left.

And maybe this
is what
you all have tried

to tell me
with your sympathetic grins
and plans,

plans *to save for the future.*

Is it time
that does this—

        or is it money:

the way we wilt into its arms
like sad children hoping

to be held for awhile.
So soon.

This seems so soon.

I remember the seed
in my blood,
        the words

alive, how love
raised a fist.

Ahh, Angela. Ahh, SDS.
Ahh, Freedom Riders.

O, revolution   never televised

ABOUT THE AUTHOR

Tim Seibles was born in Philadelphia in 1955. He has received fellowships from both the Provincetown Fine Arts Center and The National Endowment for the Arts. He also won the Open Voice Award from the 63rd Street Y in New York City. Most recently, he spent a semester as Poet in Residence at Bucknell University, a post awarded annually by the Stadler Center for Poetry. His poems have appeared in numerous literary journals including *Indiana Review, Black Renaissance Noire, Huizache, Cortland Review* and *Ploughshares*. His poem, "Allison Wolff," was anthologized in *Best American Poetry 2010*.

Tim lives in Norfolk, Virginia, where he is a member of the English Department and MFA in writing faculty of Old Dominion University. He is a teaching board member of the Muse Writers Workshop. He also teaches part-time for the University of Southern Maine's Stonecoast MFA in Writing Program, a low-residency program which features writers from all over the country.

A highly active ambassador for poetry, he presents his work nationally and internationally at universities, high schools, cultural centers, and literary festivals. He has been a featured author in the Vancouver International Writers Festival in Vancouver, Canada, in the Calabash Festival in Treasure Beach, Jamaica, and in the Poesia en Voz Alta Festival in Mexico City.

Tim Seibles is the author of six previous books of poetry.

BOOKS FROM ETRUSCAN PRESS

The Disappearance of Seth | Kazim Ali
Drift Ice | Jennifer Atkinson
Crow Man | Tom Bailey
Coronology | Claire Bateman
Cinder | Bruce Bond
Peal | Bruce Bond
Toucans in the Arctic | Scott Coffel
Body of a Dancer | Renée E. D'Aoust
Nahoonkara | Peter Grandbois
Confessions of Doc Williams & Other Poems | William Heyen
A Poetics of Hiroshima | William Heyen
Shoah Train | William Heyen
September 11, 2001, American Writers Respond | Edited by William Heyen
As Easy As Lying | H. L. Hix
Chromatic | H. L. Hix
First Fire, Then Birds | H. L. Hix
God Bless | H. L. Hix
Incident Light | H. L. Hix
Legible Heavens | H. L. Hix
Lines of Inquiry | H. L. Hix
Shadows of Houses | H. L. Hix
Wild and Whirling Words: A Poetic Conversation | H. L. Hix
Art Into Life | Frederick R. Karl
Free Concert: New and Selected Poems | Milton Kessler
Parallel Lives | Michael Lind
The Burning House | Paul Lisicky
Synergos | Robert Manzano
The Gambler's Nephew | Jack Matthews
Venison | Thorpe Moeckel
So Late, So Soon | Carol Moldaw
The Widening | Carol Moldaw
Saint Joe's Passion | JD Schraffenberger
Lies Will Take You Somewhere | Sheila Schwartz
American Fugue | Alexis Stamatis
The Casanova Chronicles | Myrna Stone
The White Horse: A Colombian Journey | Diane Thiel
The Fugitive Self | John Wheatcroft

ETRUSCAN IS PROUD OF SUPPORT RECEIVED FROM

Wilkes University

Youngstown State University

The Raymond John Wean Foundation

The Ohio Arts Council

Ohio Arts Council
A STATE AGENCY
THAT SUPPORTS PUBLIC
PROGRAMS IN THE ARTS

The Stephen & Jeryl Oristaglio Foundation

The Nathalie & James Andrews Foundation

The National Endowment for the Arts

The Ruth H. Beecher Foundation

The Bates-Manzano Fund

The New Mexico Community Foundation

The Council of Literary Magazines and Presses

Founded in 2001 with a generous grant from the Oristaglio Foundation, Etruscan Press is a nonprofit cooperative of poets and writers working to produce and promote books that nurture the dialogue among genres, achieve a distinctive voice, and reshape the literary and cultural histories of which we are a part.

etruscan press
www.etruscanpress.org

Etruscan Press books may be ordered from

Consortium Book Sales and Distribution
800.283.3572
www.cbsd.com

Small Press Distribution
800.869.7553
www.spdbooks.org

Etruscan Press is a 501(c)(3) nonprofit organization.
Contributions to Etruscan Press are tax deductible
as allowed under applicable law.
For more information, a prospectus,
or to order one of our titles,
contact us at books@etruscanpress.org.